HOW TO TREAT YOUR MAN

A BOOK FOR WOMEN

EVERYDAY ACTIONABLE TIPS FOR A HAPPY RELATIONSHIP

ANNE GRACE

CONTENTS

INTRODUCTION

When you really love someone, you want to make sure they understand how much. It might be difficult to know how to express your sentiments at times, but happily, there are several methods to express your love and devotion. Whether he's your spouse or a new lover, this essay will teach you how to love him and make the relationship endure.

Some men want vocal confirmation that their spouses love them, but others prefer to be reassured by deliberate deeds. Telling your lover you love him is essential for a good relationship.

So, if you want to show your partner that you believe he's unique, just tell him you adore him. That is something he will always want to hear. You may even surprise him with the newest iPhone or the golf club he's been yearning for. However, the most effective approach to make a guy feel loved is to do ordinary, daily acts of kindness that demonstrate that you understand him. These little gestures will reward you with a more trusting and friendly marriage, as well as a stronger feeling of connection.

We are all swept away by great gestures. In a relationship, we may place too much emphasis on pricey holidays and excursions. But, in the end, it's the little things that matter. Do you want to know how to tell your partner you love him? There are several easy methods to express the love that frequently mean much more than pricey presents or spectacular demonstrations of affection. It is not always simple to communicate your love to your spouse, whether you have been together for a long time or have just met. Take the time to express your feelings for your lover so that your relationship will remain healthy and joyful.

If you like, you may go ahead and get him a toy. Give him one of these signs of affection if you want to make him so pleased that he goes straight past "Thanks, hun" to "I've got the finest lady of my dreams." No need to go shopping.

It might be tough to put in the time and effort required to really show your lover how much he means to you. So, if you believe you have lately neglected your boyfriend, you must find a means to make up. Fortunately, there are several things you may do to show him how much you care.

CHAPTER 1

UNDERSTANDING MALE PSYCHOLOGY

There is no better place to begin your journey to understand men than here. The basic reality is that the greatest evolutionary danger to a guy is devoting his time to protecting and caring for a kid who is not his.

The greatest danger to a woman is that her boyfriend may fall in love with someone else and abandon her. It's caveman nonsense, yet the concept has been hard-coded into our minds through millions of years of evolution.

What does this have to do with understanding males in the twenty-first century? Keep an eye out. What are the guys around you afraid of? What are their interactions with other males like? What are the qualities that they value the most?

Men like feeling manly!
Men are simple beings, which I dislike speaking aloud, but women are as well. Men, like women, want to feel cared for and protected.

Men, like women, want to feel special, and they want you...their women to be the ones who make them feel special.

Recognizing men and women requires understanding that both sexes are striving toward the same objective but from different viewpoints.

Understanding this will help you understand how to transform your relationships from ordinary to life-changing.

Women often have assumptions about how men think. This is not to say that women are always correct; your perceptions and sentiments are totally acceptable. However, it's simple to misinterpret the opposing sex when you expect he should think precisely as you do. Unfortunately, he will not.

So, when comparing the female and male brains, we must begin with the assumptions women have about males: constantly thinking about sex, not listening, believing they're superior to women, not caring about how they appear, and the belief that guys don't weep. However, if you're looking for the ideal guy, it's necessary to adjust your mindset and really comprehend the subtleties of the male brain.

Here's What Women Should Know About Male
Psychology

9 Things Women Must Know About Male Psychology.

Before you have a family with the guy you now
have, learn to know him better by studying male
psychology.

1. **There is no blueprint.**
It may be tough to comprehend when it comes
to your love life and how guys think in
relationships, but there is no template for
understanding all men in all circumstances.
Even if you consult research and clinical
psychology, you'll find that men differ greatly.
While many men are terrified of intimacy or
want to take things slowly, there are some who

are hopeless romantics looking for the proper chance to settle down and build a family.

It's easy to just throw up your hands and complain that males are "just different." However, when it comes to how males approach relationships, no two guys will be precisely the same.

If you don't fully get how your male partner acts, it's not because he's a guy, but because he's not you. He is a distinct human being who does not think in the same manner that you do. You always have an option. You can locate another lover if you don't like how he thinks or treats you. But you can't make him think like you simply because you love him and believe in him.

2. Recognize that men and women are naturally and socially distinct.
Boys and girls are raised differently owing to cultural and macho stereotypes. Many guys are often praised for their daring and strong dispositions. Women, on the other hand, are often rewarded for being excellent caregivers.

According to research, parents use more language about emotions with their daughters, which promotes emotional intelligence. They, on the other hand, employ more terms about spatial things with their boys. These forms of rearing resonate in all of us, influencing the kind of people men and women grow up to be.

3. Men want space, but not usually because they are in love.

More misconceptions about men claim that guys may seem aloof when they like someone or withdraw when they fall in love. This is referred to as the rubber band effect. Even though males, like everyone else, want space, it's not a good indicator that he's lukewarm about you. He's probably having second thoughts and doesn't know how to express himself. He may even conclude that he doesn't like you, but he won't say anything until he's certain that he wants to end the relationship.

When your boyfriend or male spouse requests space, you should inquire as to what he means and why he needs it. It's okay to request this, but never make assumptions about why. Request clarification to better understand what he needs and if you can provide it. Communication is essential, but in general, a man who needs some alone time is fine; a guy who is "taking a break" from you just hasn't got

the nerve to break up with you yet. You should most likely do it for him.

4. Men are discouraged from expressing their feelings.

The stereotype that guys don't express their emotions is untrue. This is another male stereotype. Sadly, this becomes a bit of a self-fulfilling prophecy.

You may always be patient and encouraging with a person who struggles to speak up about his feelings. You may ask him questions to encourage him to express his thoughts, and you can praise him when he does, even if these sentiments are tough to hear. You may also provide him positive reinforcement when he expresses his emotions, so he understands he's safe with you.

There's a lot of discussion about males being all about their appearance, but they're truly about their sentiments.

Men want to be liked and valued. Men have the desire to be valued, even if they don't express it. When they're in a relationship, they need to feel good about themselves. If you can embrace a guy completely without criticizing or attempting to alter him, you will have a man who is thankful and loyal since no one else has ever done so.

5. Some guys are apprehensive about commitment and intimacy.
When individuals fall in love, they may sense fear. When you feel vulnerable, it might be frightening. When you fall in love, you run the risk of being harmed. Some individuals avoid

significant relationships because it is simpler to quit than to face disappointment.

Individuals with an avoidant attachment style are prone to this conduct. This type is related to the following attachment styles: secure attachment (comfortable with intimacy and being loved by others), anxious attachment (need continual attention and validation to feel loved), and avoidant attachment (avoiding intimacy subconsciously and being afraid of commitment). Men are more prone than women to develop the third.

Males are terrified of commitment, although there are 50 million willingly married men in the United States alone, while women are more inclined to shun marriage after divorce. Nonetheless, masculinity is often connected with not being vulnerable. And vulnerability entails commitment and intimacy, which may drive some men to dread and retreat.

6. Men have no idea what women desire.

Nobody knows what someone wants until they are explicitly informed.

Men, like everyone else, do not have mind-reading abilities. As a result, you must communicate your desires to them.

Talk to your spouse if you don't feel like he or she is meeting your needs or giving you what you want in your relationship. It's conceivable that he doesn't understand your expectations or wishes, in which case a chat will make all the difference. Don't expect the guy to "just know" what you're looking for.

7. The male brain is not mysterious.
Understanding male psychology does not need reading about every psychological study available. Your guy is unlike any other man. Even prevalent male behavior theories and trends (including this article!) may not apply to your mate. Outliers will always exist.

Simply said, if you want to know what a guy desires in a relationship, you should ask him. When it comes to communicating their desires, men tend to be quite straightforward and honest.

Masculine energy dislikes being directed or reprimanded. While toxic masculinity exists, not all varieties of masculinity are poisonous by nature. Competition isn't necessarily harmful. Sexuality isn't always harmful. Aggression isn't necessarily harmful. Directness isn't necessarily harmful. You know what they say about everything in moderation? However, while dealing with males in general, it's important to understand that telling men what to do is frequently a poor technique. Yes, it's a stereotype, but consider how many times you've told a guy he's wrong. What was his reaction? Most likely via his basic autonomic nerve system: fight or flight. Thus, the greatest approach to connecting with males is the same as it is with women: with validation, understanding, empathy, and curiosity - not by telling him he's wrong every time he disagrees with you.

9. Both men and women want pleasure and to avoid suffering.

This is a characteristic of human nature. Sigmund Freud, an Austrian neurologist, created the phrase "pleasure principle" to describe people's proclivity to seek pleasure and avoid suffering. He contended that individuals will go to considerable lengths to escape temporary suffering, particularly at times of psychological weakness or vulnerability. This need for pleasure explains why males would have sex without committing, and the desire to avoid suffering explains why he will not break up with you even if he does not picture himself marrying you.

It's Easier to Understand the Male Brain Than You Think
Men's psychology isn't all that difficult. Consider males to be exactly like any other human being. They, like the rest of us, want to be appreciated, listened to, cared for, challenged,

and loved. Stop obsessing about gender roles; doing so will not help you meet the right guy.

Instead of concentrating on what's wrong with guys - and trust me, there's a lot! - your best chance is to concentrate on what you can control: being cheerful, confident, and understanding with everyone you encounter along the way. It will be easy for the right guy to fall in love with you this way.

CHAPTER 2

FEMININE QUALITIES MEN LOVE

The beauty standards put on society have affected women's perceptions of femininity throughout time. However, learning how to create your best profile is dependent not on what others believe, but on how you want to be worthwhile. Always attempt to use your greatest weapons so that you don't have to rely on fantasizing about getting what you don't have. Most guys are more drawn to safety than to physical beauty. Fight to protect your attractiveness.

A woman typically has between 7 and 10 intimate partners throughout her life, compared to 9 to 12 for males. According to several well-known dating websites, the ideal average is 10. Although we feel that all resides in having a voluptuous or fit physique, the fact is that the aesthetic influence is just temporary and swiftly fades. We reveal to you the characteristics that WILL make your partners fall at your feet to make that attraction linger longer than just one date.

1. Sweetness

Nowadays, it is quite common to associate sweetness with weakness, leading many women to attempt to appear angry in order to protect themselves. It seems at first to be a means to show the world that you are someone highly valuable, but it might cause you to remain alone. A person who does not exhibit nice demeanor is undesirable to most men; just as a charming smile may make a problem vanish, an angry answer can drive away a potential partner. It is important that you strive to be yourself at all times in your life.

2. Never criticize somebody.

When you criticize someone, you are demonstrating that you are someone who enjoys speaking negatively about someone who is not in front of you. This frequently raises questions about whether you really do the same with the person in front of you or whether you are just venting on him. Try to avoid doing it in front of coworkers, relatives, or friends, since they may perceive it incorrectly. You should also keep in mind that, as much as you may like gossip, you will always end up with more knowledge if you do not rely on EVERYTHING you know about someone. It's sometimes best to keep your mouth shut.

3. Naturalness

When we imagine an ideal individual, we often picture hundreds of performers and models. But, in the end, they are not the ones who come to our aid. It is also critical that you should not pursue physical perfection, but rather that the person who ends up at your side is drawn to what you have to give. Always strive to be true to yourself and improve your look in order to feel appealing. What must happen will come when it must. Neither before nor after.

4. Intuition

One of the biggest illusions that have been nurtured over the years is that female intuition is nothing more than the capacity to grasp something thoroughly without the need for conscious thinking. As a woman, you have an intrinsic ability to recognize tensions, thus convincing him to become your ally is a piece of cake. Allow yourself to get caught away by it and learn from the times when it fails you. Everything is about knowing when to succeed and when to fail. You were born with one of the most significant gifts for many guys. Take advantage of it.

5. Independence

Men, it has been marketed through the years, prefers to safeguard their relationships. But nothing could be farther from the truth: everyone prefers to have someone by their side who can stand on their own. It does not imply that you will never have the chosen one, but that you will be able to address your own issues and pick when you will spend time with your spouse. Again, balancing is the key to avoiding being too unreachable while yet maintaining your own space.

6. Authenticity

It is important to constantly be genuine about your personality; else, your actual self will out sooner or later. If the interior does not match what you have sold, you will disappoint your partner. Simply attempt to make your qualities more pleasing than your flaws, and you will strike a balance and win over the person you have been seeking.

7. Empathy

In many circumstances, he does not necessarily wish to be "correct." He only wants to be understood. He will never really get what it is like to be a woman in this world, just as you will never fully comprehend what it takes for him to be a man. That is completely OK. However, if you can find it within yourself to acknowledge that he has a different viewpoint and to attempt to experience things through his eyes, he will be eternally grateful. This will only encourage him to reciprocate.

8. Honesty and a good sense of humor

Nothing beats a lady who is up for anything and looks good in her stilettos and his Jordans. He likes this trait since it enables him to relax his guard and lets him get rid of his obsession with constantly impressing you with fancy dates and items.

One approach to display your superior intellect is to be able to laugh at yourself. It also helps everyone around you feel at ease, making any guy feel a particular compassion for you. You must know how to use this instrument effectively to avoid being seen as a simple buddy, but if you manage to utilize the rest of your womanly weapons appropriately, you will certainly be able to win any heart that you target.

Nothing is more enticing than a lady who is content with herself, content with life... just content. A lady who often laughs, exudes pleasure and glee, and constantly brightens your day, and makes you smile anytime you see or think about her. That's the kind of person we all want to be around.

Don't get me wrong: we all have awful days, periods of uncertainty, and despair. A woman who accepts and loves herself, who knows what she wants in life and pursues it, will have much more good days than bad. She is up much more than she is down. She is upbeat, optimistic, and upbeat, and she simply makes you feel fantastic.

Your partnership should not be taken seriously all of the time. Another feature that automatically makes the connection entertaining is a sense of humor and the ability to break unexpected jokes.

It also exposes the guy to the laid-back side of your personality, which is a commendable trait. Grumpiness is an undesirable trait in women, according to men.

Humor is one of the few outstanding female attributes, since men like to spend time with women who see the humorous side of things and the reality of life rather than those who are constantly moaning.

The good news is that you don't have to be a comic genius to excel at this skill. Everything is ideal when you can connect freely with everyone, find the amusing side of things, and laugh pleasantly with him. Simply be fun and know when to be playful.

9. Passion

Passion is without a doubt one of the seductive feminine attributes that every guy seeks in addition to physical beauty.

Having a sense of purpose in life is appealing to both men and women. For males, this indicates that the female will not constantly be needy in the relationship and will not fight to fulfill her life goals.

Nothing turns guys off like a woman who is always in need. As a result, you are informing him about your other hobbies, which will put him at ease.

Men will see you as a person with fascinating traits and a lot going for you. Being enthusiastic makes him want to spend more time learning about your hidden qualities.

CHAPTER 3

WHAT MEN FIND ATTRACTIVE…(it's might not even be what you think.)

Men and women are continuously seeking for methods to attract the opposing gender, and here is where each person's individuality comes into play. Surprisingly, it is not only dependent on beauty or good looks, but also on many attributes that frequently attract individuals to one other.

This might vary depending on a number of situations, which is why Gleeden, a dating app, conducted a survey among 15,000 users in significant cities in India to determine the essential features or aspects that impact men*s experiences of overwhelming attraction towards women.

"Both men and women have numerous fascinating options for how and why they are attracted to a given sort of person. Although this varies from person to person, we were fascinated to go more into knowing what a modern guy looks for when he is attracted to women. This was a wide poll that covered men from all areas of life, and the findings were fairly intriguing in terms of how there has been a tiny change in the attributes that men are drawn to"

Sybil Shiddell

Men are intrinsically more visual searchers than women, despite the fact that women are more attracted to a man*s demeanor. The first thing a guy notices about a girl is her physical qualities, which progressively assist him understand her personality and communication style. In the aftermath of feminism, many men's opinions on how to better understand women have changed, and the poll identifies the top ten attributes that a contemporary man finds desirable in a woman.

Embracing your individuality
Men like seeing ladies in their nicest attire because it provides them a first impression of the lady they could be interested in. Outfits have their own language, so whether it's a gorgeous sundress, a stunning evening costume with heels, or even a casual outfit, dressing up nicely with hair and cosmetics leaves a lasting impact on a guy.

Being an equal
Although a man*s natural inclination to nurture his girlfriend cannot be fully eradicated, there have been some changes. Our present culture is all about equality, and things like splitting the bill on dates and making choices in a partnership as equals are absolutely a significant reason why a male would be drawn to a woman.

Taking the lead
To be honest, it is tough for males to continue to take the lead in talks or choices when you

are together. A woman who does not shy away from taking the lead and initiating on many levels is a significant turn-on for a guy and immediately makes a woman more appealing in his eyes.

Being self-assured and smiling
Nothing shines brighter than confidence and being completely at ease with yourself. A guy cannot look away from a lady who is comfortable in her own flesh. Not to mention, a nice grin goes a long way.

Women who are driven
Women are tough and powerful, and men are always delighted to watch them accomplish what they do best. They like a woman who has a strong sense of passion and an exciting enthusiasm for life, which keeps her grounded and rock solid at the same time.

Maintaining eye contact
The power of eye contact is perhaps one of the most personal things in the world. Nothing

beats the spark that eye contact provides, and when a woman maintains it with her guy, it makes him weak in the knees.

You keep him guessing.
Men enjoy the excitement of the chase and a woman's ability to keep them captivated and eager to learn more about her. Most guys find this quite appealing.

Living life to the fullest
A guy appreciates it when a woman is interested in new hobbies and is always ready for an adventure, whether it is as simple as an impromptu baking session or as exciting as trekking and trying something new with him.

Being a good listener and having intelligent dialogues
Although a woman's physical appearance is vital to any guy, he must also be able to speak with her on an intellectual level. Being with a lady who actually respects what a man has to say and cherishes him for it is something that every man seeks.

Things that are scientifically proven to make guys insane

If you've ever wondered what attracts guys the most, these seven things are the answers you've been seeking for!

1. facial symmetry

This is when the left side of your face matches the right side of your face and vice versa, with everything lining up precisely from one side to the other, and according to studies, this is also a lot more appealing.

2. Lips

According to the findings of a research conducted at Manchester University, the lips are the most beautiful physical feature of a woman.

To agree with this, think how stunning you appear, particularly while wearing red lipstick.

3. Make direct eye contact

Forget the old adage about the eyes being the window to the soul; they're also the entrance to retaining a lover's attention. It turns out that when you're attracted to someone, your pupils dilate a bit more. The clincher? People seem to be particularly drawn to dilated pupils. Lesson learned: never pass up a chance to concentrate your gaze on your desired bae.

4. Outstanding teeth

According to research, straight, white teeth are also incredibly appealing. And number 4 below explains why this is so crucial.

5. Beautiful grins

Another research reveals that males are attracted to women who smile a lot.

This is also correct, since smiling is clearly more attractive than moping and frowning. Men are substantially more attracted to women who smile. It's not like you'll be reeling them in with a frown.

6. A higher-pitched voice
High-pitched voices are presumably more appealing. According to researchers, this is because louder voices imply a smaller physical size, which our culture considers more beautiful.

7. Color red
A study of color stereotypes featured two images of the same lady. She wore blue in one photo and red in the other, posing the same manner in both. According to the findings, the picture of the lady in red was judged as more appealing and sexually desired.

This explains why red underwear is so popular.

CHAPTER 4

BEHAVIORS THAT SCARES MEN OFF

So you're dating a man, and the first few weeks are critical. You met him, exchanged phone numbers, went on your first date, and are now officially dating. You like this man and are wondering what you can do (or avoid doing) to keep this connection continuing without scaring him away.

You and your lover are overshadowed by all of the pleasure and giddiness that comes with being in a new relationship in the early stages.

He is lovely in everything he does, and vice versa. However, once the novelty of a relationship wears off, you begin to see your partner's real colors. Things he used to do may no longer be so adorable, and he may begin to see you in a new way as well.

We all have our own set of rules when it comes to dating and relationships. But what you believe is appropriate conduct may be driving your boyfriend away. As much as he wants to be with you, jumping ship and recovering his single status is beginning to appear like a better alternative.

If you've ever done any of these things in your relationship, realize that you may be making it easier for him to gather up the courage to dump you. So, if your relationship is so important to you, keep reading to find out the things you're undoubtedly doing that will drive him away for forever.

You're trash-talking your ex.

Never make fun of an ex-boyfriend in front of a man you're dating. Don't ever trash-speak your ex, whether you're on your first or fifteenth date with a man. You had a relationship with your ex. Your ex is someone you choose to be in your life. Your ex is someone you spent a lot of time with and got to know.

So don't speak adversely about your ex in any manner, because the guy you're presently seeing will hear you speak negatively about your former, and all he'll think about is himself in your ex's position one day. He will believe that if he ever becomes your ex, you would carry the same level of animosity against him and trash-speak him to other guys.

So, when a guy inquires about your ex, all you should answer is, "We are no longer together." It was a wonderful partnership that taught me a lot." That's all. Furthermore, the fact that you are continuously criticizing your ex indicates that you are not ready to move on with another relationship.

Paranoia is extreme. You're dating a guy you really adore, and things are going swimmingly for the first few weeks. Then, all of a sudden, he has a lads' night out planned with several of his coworkers. So, what are you going to do? First, before he goes out, you text him, "Have a fantastic time tonight!" You are now the cool lady you want to be.

Then, as the night goes on, the girls you're hanging out with plant seeds of doubt in your mind about what he's doing, and you begin to wonder, "Is he cheating on me?" Is he having extramarital affairs? What is he up to? "What is his current location?"

Then you commit one of the most common blunders women make: you send him another text asking him, "What's going on?" "What are you doing now?" "Having fun with my buddies," he'll remark.

Then you make a huge mistake: you start texting him often throughout the remainder of the evening to check in on him. The "checking up" will be motivated by worry that the man is doing anything other than having fun with his buddies, not by a desire to see whether he is having fun.

This kind of paranoia will drive a guy away as soon as anything else. Respecting a man's "boy time" while he's out with his pals will make you the cool lady he's always wanted to find.

Possessive and clingy.

Don't be needy or possessive. This is somewhat related to #2. Allow a guy to go out with his pals when he goes out with his friends. You are not required to accomplish everything jointly. You're still learning about him. Find out what he enjoys doing that you like doing as well, and do those things together.

But if there are things he enjoys doing that just do not interest you, accept it. For example, if you don't like to jet ski but he does, simply sit on the beach and relax while he does. You do not need to be connected at the hip.

If you're going to a cocktail party with him, you don't have to hover over him at all times. If you notice him interacting with a lady at the party, don't rush up and start grabbing his hand and hugging him. Do not, under any circumstances, do this all night. When you do this, you are becoming clinging and possessive. When you are clinging, we will want to get rid of you as soon as possible. We don't enjoy being clingy and possessive, therefore you should avoid it.

Being arrogant.

Don't behave as if you own his weekends, access to his cash, or anything else. Be polite to everyone and never treat someone as though they owe you anything.

Requiring him to pay for everything.

I'm a big admirer of courting, but don't forget to treat him well as well. Expecting him to cover everything all of the time is a bit one-sided and cruel. It might also give him the impression that you're just there for free food.

If you can't afford to pay the bill, there are other methods to show your appreciation, such as a home-cooked dinner, a date you plan, or little thoughtful surprises for him. It should seem like you're both contributing to the relationship, rather than that he's paying for your services.

Having No Life

It's tempting to want to spend every waking minute with your significant other, but spending too much time with your mate is never a good thing. If your main social life is with him, you're in for a harsh surprise. Your active social life was most likely what drew him to you when you first met him. He had no idea when he'd see you again, and the unpredictability of your connection was really a nice thing. It made the time you spent together that much more enjoyable.

But now that you've given up all of your pals and activities, life has become monotonous and complacent. He knows you'll want to spend every weekend with him, and he's reached the point where he truly needs a break.

If you've been ignoring your pals and no longer making time to see individuals who aren't your boyfriend, it's time to get in shape before it's too late. No man wants to be a woman's whole universe. So, get out of your relationship as soon as possible.

Attempting to Change Him

Your man has a history with women who have attempted to alter him at some time. Maybe his ex attempted to get him to stop playing video games, or maybe his admirer offered to date him only if he dropped a few pounds. Some women may seem to be OK with the way their spouse is, but as time passes, they will strive to modify the way he behaves, his clothes, his friends, his work, and so on.

Everyone wants to be accepted for who they are, and your man is no exception. It's perfectly OK to push him to improve his eating habits and to offer him advice on how to progress in his work. But if you create the impression that he's not good enough for you, he'll begin to drift away.

You're in for an unpleasant surprise if you believe nagging and criticizing him would make him alter his ways.

Early push for commitment.
It's nice to know where a possible relationship is headed at all times. Guys will feel pressured to commit if you query them too often and too early on.

So, when is it appropriate to have "the talk?" To be honest, there is no "proper" moment; it should occur spontaneously.

If he likes you, he will bring up the subject and commit. Remember that you can always walk away if things aren't going the way you want them to.

No Trust.

Men's minds have evolved to convince them that they should be competent and that if they're REAL guys, women will trust them. There are several subtle methods to convey that you do not trust a guy. They are as follows:

Taking control of what he is doing or should be doing

He was constantly questioning him about his location.

Doubts about his capacity to manage other women who want him

Criticizing his methods because they are not your methods

If you find yourself doing these things, consider how you feel when a guy follows you around, searches your phone, or undermines your capacity to accomplish anything. Doesn't it feel bad when your spouse behaves in a manner that makes you feel distrusted? Indeed, it soon leads to bitterness and a significant emotional distance in the partnership.

Trust your guy to make his own judgments, and even if he makes mistakes, he'll know you've got his back. Allow him to do what he wants and live his life according to his own set of rules. Encourage him to spend time with his friends and avoid interrogating him in a manner that implies you already suspect him of wrongdoing. There's a considerable difference between genuine interest in his night out and disguised efforts to 'find him out.'

Train your thoughts to initially give him the benefit of the doubt, particularly if you've been harmed before by untrustworthy guys. Why are you with a person if you don't trust him because he is dishonest or incapable of following through on his words with actions?

CHAPTER 5

THINGS MEN WANTS BUT WON'T TELL YOU

We've all become used to males making direct pronouncements. And it's one of the primary factors in distinguishing between men and women. Of course, you may consider yourself a female with a guy mentality, preferring to spend out with males since ladies are difficult, and so on. Immediacy and simplicity simplify our lives and relationships, but what if I told you that guys don't always speak what they think, particularly in important partnerships? Yes, men do not always articulate their preferences in a relationship. But why keep it hidden? The only response that is possibly true is that males don't know about their own wants until they obtain them from women.

One significant difference between men and women that I've seen is that women appear to be far more aware of what they want and need in a relationship...and aren't hesitant to voice it. For different reasons, men aren't always in touch with what they really need in a relationship to feel loved and happy, and those who are are seldom vocal about it.

From an academic viewpoint, it makes sense. Women learn at a young age how to create tight, personal connections, as well as what makes them feel cared for and understood. Because male friendships lack the same depth and intimacy, males often join the domain of emotional awareness later in life, usually when they start connections with women.

A man won't usually ask for what he needs since he doesn't always know what it is. But when you give it to him, it feels incredible. He feels valued and adored, and he grows to adore you even more.

Subconsciousness is quite important in this aspect, and sometimes all it takes is a little study to practically penetrate a guy's head. Some of these behaviors may not only attract a guy's attention, but they may also strengthen your relationship and make your partner happier. You will definitely feel appreciated in no time! Let's find out what the key things are that every male wants his lady to do but doesn't tell her.

Show him your appreciation. This is the number one thing that all males secretly want from a relationship, but not all ladies understand what it means. Take action and demonstrate to your lover that his opinions, choices, and emotions are important.

Your guy will ALWAYS need your love and respect, just as you do. Learn his love language and make an effort to communicate it to him on a regular basis. Touch him often and observe this to grasp its significance. Compliment him on things he does for you on a regular basis.

There is no scenario in which your guy will not appreciate receiving additional love and admiration from you in the manner he prefers to get it, even if the actions he took to earn it seem conventional or boring. The problem is that this is one of the most difficult things to ask for since it might make you feel uneasy.

If you find it difficult to show him love and affection, it's possible that you've lost sight of why you felt that way in the first place. This occurs when the routines and problems of life become more important than the actual relationship itself. Redirecting your focus to the vital things in life can restore your natural sentiments of love for your guy.

Compliments

No guy will ever come out and say he appreciates it when you compliment him because it's a strange thing to ask for, and it's also not very "manly," if you will. But just because he doesn't ask doesn't mean he doesn't want anything.

Men, like women, are self-conscious about their physical appearance, and they don't get nearly as much affirmation as we do. Consider this: when a man shares a photo on Facebook or goes out with pals, he doesn't have a devoted following remarking on how good he looks. You're actually his sole source of praise for his physical looks, so fill him up! See him that clothing looks hot on him, that you can tell he's been working out hard at the gym, that a specific color draws attention to his eyes, that his hair looks attractive pulled back... you get the idea!

Solicit for his advice/guidance.

It's a terrific method to show your partner that his opinion counts when you're unsure about something crucial. A guy privately wants to know that his ideas are important to you and that you value his comments.

You know how wonderful it feels when your boyfriend appreciates, adores, and lavishes you with love? When you ask for his guidance, he feels the same way. Men have an overpowering want to feel helpful as if they have something valuable to give. This is true in many aspects of his life, but particularly in his relationships. He wants to feel like he's making a difference in your life, and you may help him feel that way by requesting his thoughts and views.

Men, in general, are solution-oriented and flourish when there is a problem to solve. That's why, when you talk to a man about something that's bothering you, he'll usually try to solve your problems, which most women find frustrating because all we really want in those moments is emotional support, and men don't realize that giving said support is more of a solution to the problem than actually solving the problem! (And if your husband does this, don't get upset at him; instead, tell him you appreciate his counsel but need his emotional support right now.)

Make him feel valued.

Always remember to thank your boyfriend for a fun night out at the restaurant. Reward him with a grin or kiss to show him how much you appreciate what he does for you. But don't go overboard.

Appreciation is undoubtedly the most powerful incentive for a guy, yet it is something that most men lack. To maintain your relationship joyful and meaningful, you must show gratitude for all he does, large and little. Men, as previously said, need your praise and need to feel like victors. When you show real gratitude, you are striking two birds with one stone and giving him the most valuable present you can offer. The worst thing you can do is demand things from him or appear entitled to them.

It's not only about what he does for you; it's also about recognizing who he is. Thank him for his positive characteristics, ideals, objectives, and life choices. Find the qualities you like in him and express your gratitude. Don't simply assume he knows, since he doesn't. This is most likely the most powerful and transforming relationship skill you will ever learn.

Take action and demonstrate your passion for him.

You don't have to wait for your boyfriend to make physical contact with you. Do not conceal your feelings and act just when you feel like it. It is an instant turn-on for any male.

You don't have to wait for him to initiate physical affection all of the time. Men like feeling irresistible—as if you're turned on by him and can't get enough of him—so flirt with him, entice him, and start physical connection. Seeing how turned on his girlfriend is by him is a major turn-on for a guy!

CHAPTER 6

SECRETS TO GETTING A MAN TO OPEN UP

"I have no idea what he's thinking since he never tells me anything."

Does this sound familiar? According to a recent research, 42 percent of couples have difficulty persuading their spouse to disclose his thoughts. When this occurs, she feels alone, and he feels misunderstood. But, as a therapist and author, I've uncovered something that many women are unaware of. Men desire to converse. They'll chat all night if the circumstances are good. Most guys are anxious to unburden themselves.

So, what is the trick to persuading your man to share? Continue reading—and brace yourself for an earful.

Secret 1: Real men are terrified of rejection—truly!

That is correct. Most guys believe that women are highly critical of them, and they are afraid that if they open themselves, someone would laugh at them, rejecting and humiliating them. Women must understand that a man's ego and sense of identity are often more vulnerable and quickly damaged than hers. This is particularly true in personal relationships: he seeks acknowledgment, feedback, and the knowledge that he has delighted you. So, if a guy believes that you are going to condemn him or look at him differently as a consequence of what he says, he will not speak.

Allowing your spouse to communicate what is on his mind and merely being open to hear it means not criticizing him. This does not exclude you from having an opinion or from expressing it at some time. To open up to you, he needs to be fully welcomed for who he is, not who you want him to be. Be kind with him. If you reply to his views by providing your point of view right away with anything like "That is incorrect. "I disagree," or "Where did you acquire such a strange idea? "Any guy will immediately clam up. They are worried that if they say anything too intimate, it would contradict the picture you have of them, or the image they push themselves to present.

A guy might be many different things at various times in his life—even during the week or day. Don't be hesitant to let him show you various sides of himself. If you can let go of your expectations and simply attempt to figure out who he is, he will notice it right away, feel at peace, and enjoy talking to you.

Secret 2: Reveal yourself.

Mutual transparency is required between partners. Everyone has issues, worries, and skeletons in their closet. Many men believe that "if I disclose this, she'll leave me." You must demonstrate that this is not the case by exposing something about yourself that demonstrates that you have as much faith in him as he has in you.

When he begins to open up, listen to what he has to say before going a step further and offering something nice in response. Say something like, when he tells you something personal, "That's not so horrible, is it? I've done far worse." "I genuinely appreciate this about what occurred," and then choose something in the tale that you absolutely admire. (However, don't make this up. It'll fall flat and devolve into manipulation. People are always aware when they are being influenced on some level, and it never ends well.) Let him know you're on his side and that he's not alone in his struggle.

Make certain that you take his side while providing comments. Many women listen to men's experiences only to reply by informing him how he's been looking at things incorrectly. They take someone else's side. In a work-related narrative, for example, it may be a difficult colleague. It is critical, however, that you consider the problem from his perspective. This is not the time to instruct or train him; rather, this is the moment to "become friends." When two individuals become friends, they share their similar experiences and feel closer and more comfortable as a result. You're establishing rapport here, the impression that the two of you share the same planet and live in a similar environment.

It's incredible how many males feel completely alone. Not only have they been schooled to be silent, taught that expressing their feelings is unmanly, but they seldom get response from the males in their society. Your candid and positive feedback is essential. If you connect in this manner, your partner will feel that there is someone who understands them and will open up even more.

Third Secret: Let Go of the Past

Have you ever had a "conversation" with your spouse that turned into a slew of old grudges, things he did wrong, ways he damaged you, and what he owes you now? It occurs at some time in almost every relationship, but the truth remains that men squirm when they sense something is about to happen.

It is hard for a guy to open himself when he is afraid that his comments may be misinterpreted, misconstrued, told to others, or flung back at him. And the only way out of this communication quagmire is to recognize that whatever occurred in the past, whatever he did or said, you were also engaged. Every partnership is a dance. Nobody is wholly nice or totally evil. In reality, rather than seeing somebody as good or terrible, it is more instructive to observe the roles that are being played in the relationship and the ways in which we all get locked in patterns that we don't know how to break.

Some women, for example, like portraying the sufferer or martyr. They need the relationship's blame to legitimize their own sentiments and to feel dominant over their spouse. In reality, girls may cling to a guy in this manner for a time. However, it is a solid indicator that communication has entirely stopped and the relationship is on the rocks.

Try this if you wish to prevent or improve this unfortunate situation and help him communicate to you honestly. Accept responsibility for your role in the circumstance and consider how you may have contributed to what occurred. This does not imply that you should blame yourself. Simply taking a broad view of the matter. Consider all of the things he did "good," rather than "bad." If you need more guidance, get out your diary and write a list of what you've gotten from the relationship and what you've given in return. Consider occasions when you were less than ideal, as well as the ways in which you have both grown and changed.

Secret 4: Become a Stable and Safe Listener

Is it really possible to build trustworthy relationships? The presumption is that everyone will be truthful. The fact is that very few individuals are. And the major reason individuals are dishonest is because the repercussions are too severe. Many males believe that women desire and need to be lied to because they are incapable of accepting the truth. Some of my clients have expressed concern about giving their spouse the truth about their circumstances or how they genuinely feel for fear of upsetting her. Indeed, many women utilize their emotions to exert control over men—and hence the relationship. They expect specific answers from guys and are disappointed if they do not get them. They are startled when he closes down and does not speak.

Unfortunately, many women have preconceived notions about how a guy is "supposed" to feel and think. Because that type of dream makes the reality terrible, women make it clear to the guy in a variety of subtle ways that they do not want it. Does this sound familiar? We're all guilty of it from time to time, but being open to hearing what he has to say is the start of a genuinely mature relationship. It offers the guy the impression that he has a reliable companion who will stick with him through thick and thin.

If you're ready to get out of this unrealistic rut, ask yourself three questions. How much truth are you willing to accept? How much do you really desire? Do you want your boyfriend to be a dream figure for you, or do you want him to become real to you? These are significant questions. You may not be able to accept all of the truth at once, but you can surely strengthen your tolerance muscles and go in that direction.

Surprisingly, we all believe that imagination makes us feel good, yet the more reality we can handle, the stronger we become. As we recognize that genuine security comes not from the acceptance of others, but from being truthful to ourselves, our capacity to tolerate honesty from others grows.

5th Secret: Be Yourself—Be Aware

It's an old but valid question. How can we be honest with someone if we aren't honest with ourselves? The easiest method to assist a guy open up is to just be open yourself, to be natural, to be true, and to emanate a loving and accepting environment. Those we meet in life are reflections of various aspects of ourselves, and we attract individuals who each help us love a different aspect of ourselves.

This is why the five themes discussed here should be applied not just to the males in our lives, but also to ourselves. For example, can you let go of self-judgment? Do you disregard previous complaints about things you've done wrong? Or do you constantly fixate on your errors and where you've fallen short? It is only natural to treat your mate the same way you treat yourself. If you were constantly punished or made to feel inadequate as a child, you are likely to do the same to your boyfriend.

It is critical to be aware in this situation. If you want to build a more open dynamic between your spouse and yourself, take a thorough inventory of how you treat and value yourself, as well as how you were handled by previous significant others. If you have been harmed, now is the time to decide that you will no longer spend your life as an automatic pilot. Flip it around. Decide to be kind and accepting of yourself and the person you're with.

We sometimes give in to others in the hope of obtaining the same in return. When it doesn't happen, quiet rage begins to rise. That is acting with an agenda, sending contradictory signals, and not being authentic to yourself or others. To fully give of oneself, you must recognize that you "get" as much from giving as you do from getting. When you offer someone absolute respect and consideration, you are also giving it to yourself. You're acting in the greatest manner possible, and the good vibes always come back to you. When you treat people with respect, you are instilling a feeling of value and worth in them. Though your spouse does not reciprocate, you will not feel as if it is your fault or loss. Instead, you'll quickly move on to someone more like you.

The basic line is to be genuine to yourself because it is infectious. The guys (and women) you are with will begin to act similarly. They will talk honestly and organically, without any preconceived notions of manipulation or control. If they do not act in this manner, they will naturally leave your life—to a location that is more suitable for them.

CHAPTER 7

PERSONAL QUESTIONS TO ASK A GUY (THAT WILL REALLY MAKE HIM OPEN UP!)...just to spice things and connect deeply.

It's becoming more difficult to form meaningful connections in an era where texting is the primary way of communication and we use emoticons and memes to express ourselves. Many of us are terrified of being vulnerable, and there are certain areas we just would not go... very few recognize that this is why so many individuals struggle to form meaningful bonds. Whether you've been in a relationship with your boyfriend for a long and want to discover more about him to help you determine if he's the one for you, asking a lot of questions may be either enlightening or irritating - so proceed with care.

Rather than bombarding him with questions to ask a man, try approaching him with some classic inquiries that will make him feel at ease and allow him to open up a little.

Despite having more access to people because to technology, it is now more difficult to get to know someone since we are all so distracted by the same technology that is intended to bring us closer together. Sometimes you have to put in more effort to connect with males on a deeper level, and asking these questions to a man is a wonderful approach to gather the information you need to help you determine whether he's the perfect person for you.

To make the most of your talks, don't only ask a question; ask follow-up questions as well.

You'll be best buddies before you know it if you go through them!

1. How Do You Feel Most Loved?

Learning how he feels loved can help you connect more deeply and effectively. It will also take much of the guessing out of what he requires from you.

You may believe you're giving him affection, but if it's in a manner that he doesn't appreciate (or is even skeptical of), your relationship may struggle to progress.

On the other side, by expressing affection in the ways he needs, you may make him feel comfortable and valued.

2. What do you consider to be a healthy relationship?

Find out what he considers to be healthy and what his expectations are for the relationship. You may also ask him who has modeled a relationship in his life that he admires. Ask him why he admires their connection and whether he sees it occurring for you two.

3. What is your pet project?

Discover what is important to him and how he spends his time. When you learn about his interests, convey your want to share them with him. Don't forget to acknowledge his enthusiasm! He may have had partners in the past who ignored his 'hobbies' or made fun of what he was passionate about.

You have the chance to encourage and build him up.

4. What is one item that always makes you grin, no matter what time of day it is?

5. Do you wish you could go back in time and alter something?

6. How do you deal with stress?

7. Do you become easily enraged?

8. Do you believe that men and women should be treated equally?

9. Which TV character do you most identify with?

10. What one aspect of yourself would you alter if you could?

11. What is one item/thing you are very proud of?

12. What causes you to laugh?

13. What is your go-to Netflix program when you're feeling particularly lazy?

14. What is the most terrifying thing you've ever done?

15. What is your favorite childhood memory?

16. What is the finest thing about your current situation?

17. What is one item/thing you are grateful for?

18. What is your greatest fear?

19. What movie would you watch if you could only watch one for the rest of your life?

20. Can you tell me anything, no matter how big or tiny, that you've never told anybody else?

21. If you were forced to leave your house and relocate to a new county, what three items would you bring with you?

22. What is your fondest memory with a pet/animal?

23. In your family, who are you closest to?

24. How would you describe your family?

25. What is your favorite ice cream flavor?

26. Tell me about your favorite joke.

27. What is the dumbest thing you've ever done?

28. If you could alter one thing about your history, what would it be?

29. What do you believe is your finest physical feature?

30. What is one aspect of your personality that you admire?

31. Who or what is your go-to person or activity when you're feeling down?

32. What would you eat if you could only eat one meal for the rest of your life?

33. What is one thing you are really enthusiastic about?

34. If you had to give up one of your five senses, what would it be and why?

35. What is the most physically demanding thing you've ever done?

36. What is the most difficult thing you've ever done or gone through mentally?

37. What is your favorite aspect of your job?

38. What is one thing that identifies you?

39. What would you do in your final 24 hours if tomorrow was your last day on Earth?

40. What are your general or religious beliefs?

41. If you were to sum up your personality in three words, what would they be?

42. What is the coolest spot you've ever visited or gone to?

43. What makes you the most embarrassed?

44. How was your first relationship?

45. What was your worst day ever?

46. What was your most memorable day?

47. Have you ever experienced the loss of someone close to you?

48. Have you ever developed an addiction to something?

49. What is the most heinous lie you've ever told?

50. What is something you usually put off?

51. Do you believe in soulmates?

52. Are you hesitant to express your feelings?

53. When was the last time you shed a tear?

54. In your life, who do you have the greatest faith in?

55. Do you get along well with your father?

56. Do you believe that owning a cat is feminine?

57. What do you want to be in 20 years?

58. What would your ideal day entail?

59. Do you follow a system of rules in your life?

60. What do you believe is humanity's most serious problem?

61. Do you believe you've ever faced discrimination?

62. What is the significance of your faith to you?

63. What causes you stress?

64. Have you ever gone to visit a therapist? Or did you intend to? Why haven't you done so?

CHAPTER 8

HOW TO TREAT YOUR MAN (THE TIPS)

Make sincere compliments/praises to him.

Ladies like it when men notice their new hairstyle, fragrance, heels, alluring clothes, and other characteristics. They soon forget that guys like such little compliments as well.

Taking the time to appreciate the tiny things about your partner demonstrates your interest in him.

You don't have to save your praises for noticeable improvements like new clothes or aftershave. You may create an impression by making little remarks on a few qualities you like, such as the sparkle in your man's eyes or the noticeable dimples that appear when he grins.

Most women notice and appreciate little details about a guy they adore, but only a few will go out of their way to tell him about it.

Make him happy with himself.
You may absolutely say things like "You're so gorgeous" or "You have the prettiest grin," but you can also go deeper and tell him what you actually admire about him. Say something unique that shows him you care. Never take your love for granted and never assume that your boyfriend understands how you feel about him. He should always know that you admire and adore him for who he is. "You're very amazing at helping me feel better after I've had a difficult day," for example.

"It's incredible that you're so committed to running despite your hectic schedule. I wish I could be that driven!"

"You do realize you have the ability to make practically anybody on the earth laugh, don't you?"

Genuine comments on his appearance and strength demonstrate that you like him, which translates to love." Mention how much you appreciate having such a strong guy around when he easily opens the lid on the jam jar. He'll be happy, we promise.

Make an offer to massage him.

Giving your partner a romantic massage is a wonderful, private method to express your love for him. It will assist him in relaxing and letting go of any stress (and maybe even get him turned on).

Make a relaxing setting for your boyfriend's massage. Your bedroom will be alright; just be sure to put down a towel first to preserve the covers. Dim the lights and put on some relaxing music.

Ask him to undress (though he may keep his underwear on if he chooses) and lay face down on the bed. Begin at his feet and work your way up his legs, back and shoulders, neck, and top of his head. Firm pressure and lengthy, soothing strokes are recommended. More detailed tips on how to offer an excellent massage may be found here.

Use massage oil to avoid tugging or pinching his skin and instead allow your hands to glide softly over his flesh. You may purchase a massage oil or just use whatever sunflower or grapeseed oil you have on hand.

Examine him in the eyes.

You don't have to look at each other wistfully like you used to with your 9th-grade lover at the roller rink. Just take a minute to gaze each other in the eyes and exchange a glance.

If you believe cliches about what males prefer, a soul-gazing connection would not be on his list of desirable qualities, but I defy you to try it. Hold his stare for three seconds with a grin or a humorous look in your eyes. It's an effective flirting tactic for singles since it makes the other person feel like the only one in the room. He may be your boyfriend or spouse today, but he needs to be treated with respect.

Put on your best outfit. It's no secret that guys are highly visual beings, so getting dolled up and looking nice can be a huge turn-on.

What gets your guy moving, on the other hand, is a matter of personal choice. Some males love ladies dressed in tight, flesh-baring outfits, while others prefer a more toned-down casual approach.

The most essential thing is that you don't lounge about the home in your sweats and unclean hair (at least not constantly). You want to show him that you care about your looks and want to look well for him.

Keep your hair clean and tidy, apply a wonderful moisturizer to your skin, wear a scent he enjoys, and dress in clothing that compliments your body and showcases your finest qualities.

Don't overdo it on the make-up, but a little mascara (to make your eyes sparkle) and non-sticky lip balm (to promote kissability) will help you appear your best.

Capture his attention. Smile. Repeat.

Giving your spouse a million pleasant tiny moments with you is essential to a long-lasting relationship, and he should reciprocate. After all, research reveals that the level of friendliness between couples seems to be the most important factor in a good marriage.

Even though I attempted to make it seem thus, it's not always simple to do some of these tasks. They sometimes force us to be vulnerable in ways we aren't accustomed to. I understand; I've been there, and occasionally I still am. But I believe it is worthwhile to give it a chance.

And inquire about his list of little things that make him happy; I'm sure you're already doing many of them.

Send him a love letter.
Show him how much you care by doing something out of the ordinary. Cook his favorite dinner while he is away and have it ready by the time he arrives. Take his favorite sweets with you to the checkout line and surprise him when you get home. You may even plan a night out on the town for him by booking a reservation at his favorite restaurant.
Even if there is no specific occasion, surprise him. This will make him feel really special.

Display your affection in his preferred language.

People express and want to be loved in many ways. The five love languages might assist you in determining how to adore your spouse. Words of affirmation, acts of service, gifts, quality time, and physical contact are examples of these. Discuss with your spouse how he prefers to express and receive love, or experiment with various methods to express your love and watch how he reacts. [4]

If your partner's love language is words of affirmation, make it a point to tell him often what you like about him.

Try doing anything to make your partner's hectic day a bit easier as an act of service. Do the dishes or offer to clean the flat while he naps.

Gifts might range from flowers to a brand new sweater.

Making one-on-one plans together might be a simple way to spend quality time. Even if you're both really busy, make time for each other by planning a date night.

When he needs it, strengthen him.

Your boyfriend may want a little pep talk from time to time. He might be unhappy because of a career failure or a disagreement with his friends and family. Step in to be his cheerleader and restore his confidence in himself. Tell him that he can achieve everything he desires or that the setback he had is easily overcome. He may not request that you help him feel better, but try to understand when he really needs your assistance.

Use phrases like, "I know you're unhappy because someone else received the promotion, but I know you'll be OK. You're really brilliant and powerful!"

If he is uncertain about accomplishing a future goal, encourage him to strive "Never, ever question yourself. I'm certain you'll excel at everything you set your mind to."

Respect him.

First and first, if you're committed to a guy you don't respect, you need to look in the mirror and ask yourself why you'd want to do so.

More significantly, there is nothing more fundamental to the sustainability of your partnership than respect. You don't want to offer your spouse respect just because he wants it. You wish to express your feelings for him by showing respect. Nagging him, invalidating his thoughts, delivering non-constructive criticism, and probing him because of your own trust concerns are all examples of little acts that do not demonstrate respect.

This certainly applies in both directions. Even if you don't like what your spouse does or if the two of you stop talking due to an emotional separation, you may get things back on track if you still show respect for each other. Even if you can't, you'll look back and be pleased with how you behaved.

This also summarizes how to comprehend what guys want from women. If you can be proud of how you behave and try your best to look beyond yourself to your partner's needs as well, you're on the right track to lasting attraction and love.

Avoid making him feel inferior or horrible about himself. Respect his viewpoint, even if it sometimes varies from yours. Thank him for going out of his way to assist you. Avoid talking about him behind his back or making fun of him in groups. Respect is an important aspect of sincerely loving someone. Treat him the way you would want to be treated. It's crucial to keep in mind that individuals may be quite sensitive, and you never want to harm your man's emotions.

Pay attention to him.

Hearing what a guy has to say is a crucial element of loving him. If he's talking to you, don't interrupt or wait for the right moment to say anything. Listen to him, even if he doesn't open up to you as much as you'd want. You'll get a feel of what he wants after he's done his piece—either advice or simply a sympathetic ear.

Listening is a talent that may be taught. Work on remembering the specifics of what he says and mentioning them afterward. He'll be impressed by your concern.

Accept him just as he is.

Try not to alter him. Sure, you and your guy may help each other become better individuals in the long term, but you must remain loyal to yourself. If you really love your guy, you must accept him for who he is. You can undoubtedly assist him to improve a few characteristics, but you should love him for who he is, not who you think he will become.

If you attempt to modify him, he'll catch on quickly. It might make him feel wounded or as if he isn't good enough for you.

Express your thanks.

Tell him how grateful you are for your wonderful connection. Don't assume he understands you're thankful because you've been around so long. Take the time to tell him how much you enjoy spending time with him and thank him for all he does for you. This will show him that you really love him and value the time you spend together. [8] Here are some examples of what you might say:

"I consider myself very fortunate to have met someone as unique as you. I can't fathom how difficult it must be for all of my single friends to find someone half as wonderful as you..."

"I can't believe I came upon you. Aren't we both fortunate to have each other?"

"I'm always reassured by the knowledge that I have you in my life, no matter how horrible my day at work is. At the end of the day, all I can say is that I'm grateful to have someone like you at my side."

Of course, he should express his appreciation to you.

Give him your whole attention.

"When the male brain sees you checking your iPhone over dinner, it perceives it as 'I'm not important,'" marriage therapist Mike Dow, explains that this is because men's brains evolved to accomplish one thing at a time while filtering out all other information. Even though women work differently, your guy enjoys it when you give him your undivided attention. "It communicates, 'You are my priority, and I adore you,'" explains Dr. Dow. So keep eye contact with him and minimize disruptions.

Seek his counsel.

Your boyfriend wants to feel that he is a vital part of your life and that his thoughts are valued. Ask for his advice on how to approach your supervisor for a raise, and you'll demonstrate that you respect and appreciate his opinion. "Asking for guidance demonstrates that you trust him and that he has a role in your life. Need, reliance, and love all go hand in hand

Respectfully address disagreements.

Disagreements should be resolved openly and frankly. If he's doing anything that irritates you, choose a moment when you're both available to chat and bring it up calmly. Use I-statements to express your point of view without assigning blame. This will allow him to hear your point of view without becoming defensive. If he comes to you with a problem, fully listen to his point of view before defending yourself or explaining your actions.

When it comes to relationships, no one is flawless. If you make a mistake, accept responsibility and apologize. He'll appreciate your candor and believe you value him more as a result.

The latest workplace drama or family feud affects him emotionally more than he'd care to admit. So provide a safe haven for your boyfriend to let down his guard. " Listen to his concerns or difficulties without attempting to solve them." It demonstrates to him that you do not see him as weak or insufficient, and it gives him a space in the relationship to express that aspect of his life. It also demonstrates that you care." If he arrives home from work in a foul mood, ask him if he wants to vent. If not, that's OK — but he may need a nudge to get the floodgates open.

If the discussion becomes hot, take a pause so that you can both cool down. Wait until both of you can resolve the disagreement in a calm, sympathetic manner.

Don't expect him to be able to read your thoughts. It is better to express your emotions directly. He may be willing to adjust what he's been doing or accommodate your sentiments, but he won't know how until you tell him.

Your self-assurance will astound him.

Being happy and confident with yourself is a terrific approach to adoring a guy. This will help him appreciate you more and make him feel that your relationship is beneficial to both of you, rather than like he needs to spend all of his time putting you up. Working on liking yourself, your body, what you do, and who you surround yourself with can help all of your relationships. The sooner you accept who you are, the better you and everyone around you will feel.

Demonstrate to him that you don't require his approval to feel good about yourself. You should be content following your own interests, socializing with your friends, and having a good time without him.

Nobody is flawless. It's critical to be aware of your flaws so that you can address them, but you can also love yourself.

Look out for yourself.

Reducing stress, eating correctly, exercising, quitting smoking, and even pampering yourself may seem like pleasures, but they're also methods to show him how much you care."

This says, 'I want to live a long, great life with you, and I'll do whatever it takes to save you from going through the agony of losing someone.' What greater reason do you need to go to the gym?

Put on the outfit he adores.
Dressing up for him conveys the message that you still want to appear well for him, no matter how long you've been together. Dr. Dow claims that "men's brains are structured to react to visual stimuli more than women's brains." "Seeing you in that sexy dress shows him how much you want

him." Consider wearing a red dress as your go-to option. According to a study conducted by researchers at the University of Rochester in New York, ladies in red are an aphrodisiac to men.

Show Interest in Him, Too

While it is true that men like the chase, this cycle becomes the dynamic of the relationship when you allow it to continue and refuse to do any of the efforts yourself. The difficulty is that once you start enjoying a man and don't want to seem indifferent longer, you've created a dynamic in which you can't reveal it. He will stop pursuing and working if you do. If you don't, you'll spend the rest of your relationship playing games.

It's all about finding a happy medium and realizing that there's a vast difference between expressing interest in your partner and anxiously 'chasing' him. He still needs to know that you will return his calls, that you will find time in your schedule to see him, and that you will have a good time with him. He wants you to be interested in his life and what drives him. Be cautious not to mistake 'chasing' behavior, such as sending 20 SMS in a day, demonstrating real interest in order to make him feel desired.

Touch him to express your feelings.

Give your boyfriend an intimate touch now and again. Touching your boyfriend every day, whether it's placing your hand on his arm or kissing him on the cheek, is essential for developing your relationship. Even if you've arrived home from work tired, a little touch will make you two feel more connected. Try cuddling in the mornings or simply touching each other as much as possible. This will undoubtedly demonstrate your affection for him. Maybe your partner isn't into a lot of PDAs. When you reach home, you may still give him a quick peck on the cheek or embrace. Choose a lingering embrace over a quick peck before running out the door in the morning. " While women engage verbally, males connect more via touch, according to research "For at least seven seconds, hug. It's a long time, but there's something about that number that makes the hold really work for him." And there's no doubt you'll like it as well.

Make time for sexiness.

In many couples, sex is really significant. Make time for some bedroom entertainment (when you're in the mood, of course). It's easy to put off sex because you're exhausted or have too much work to accomplish, but scheduling sex at least once or twice a week will make both of you feel more connected. It also helps you feel better! Do it not just for him, but also for yourself. It will bring you two closer together.

Making love for a few minutes has feel-good effects. "I hope that the majority of your lovemaking is filled with foreplay and romance. But sometimes you just want to have sex." Men have a boost in dopamine, a chemical released after sex that activates the cerebral pleasure-and-reward center, whereas women have similar love sensations when they produce oxytocin during a post-sex cuddle session.

Many couples who have been together for a long time get into the same tedious lovemaking pattern. Experiment with having sex at a different time or location anytime you like.

Encourage him to devote some time to himself.

While you may not be afraid to request personal time, your spouse may have difficulty expressing his wants. Suggest that he take a day to relax with friends, play video games, work on his car, or simply sleep in. "This shows support and gives him the freedom to be his best self," clinical psychologist Andra says. This worry-free and chore-free time will be viewed by your husband as a loving reward from an amazing wife.

People need to unwind with their friends every now and then. There is nothing wrong with that, just as there is nothing wrong with wanting to spend time with your friends. Don't be wary the next time he makes arrangements with his mates. If you're okay with letting him hang out with his pals on occasion, he'll appreciate you much more when he returns to you.

Keep the flame burning.

Make it feel new, no matter how long you've been dating. On your date nights, put on something nice. Before you leave for work, leave him romantic notes. Send him adorable text messages. Purchase a tiny present for him just because you are thinking about him. If you really want to love your partner, you must constantly work for it (and he must also strive for it).
Even if you don't have to play hard to get if you're truly happy together, you should never become complacent in your relationship. Always keep things intriguing, novel, and unique.

Keep your relationship fresh by trying new things together, such as traveling to new places or taking up new hobbies. It's critical to keep things fresh if you want to truly love your man!

CONCLUSION

As a woman treating your man nicely has to come from within, that's the only way to get into him, your connection level with him will make it easier for you. So while you carry out the information in this book you need to be patient and understand that what you want from your man as a woman is probably some of the things he wants from you but his masculine ego won't let him ask. Men are big babies, they love to be treated like one. A man loves his mother more because no matter what he does or how old he gets, his mother will always pamper and treat him as if he was a child. So try your best but be ensure to know your stand in his life before you give in that best.

Made in United States
Troutdale, OR
12/08/2024

26064585R00066